HELLO

This book is about connecting to your resilience and inner strength in a creative and playful way. The dark times we went through triggered us to channel our emotions into The Warrior Sisters' stories. The "inbetween" was a transformational time for us to escape, to give something back to ourselves and to reset our lives.

Like magpies, we gathered tips and tools which we used to inspire and strengthen us. We want to share what we've learned with other women so it can help them too. We hope this book will help you, and that in reading it, you'll want to share it with other Warrior women you know.

"Inbetween" is a special space where you can explore, connect to and appreciate yourself.

Consider this a *best friend in your pocket*.

You will be introduced to 12 female archetypes; *The Warrior Sisters*.

Throughout your own "inbetween" moments, make friends with each Warrior Sister in all her shapes and forms. Share her wisdom and strength and *be empowered*.

How to use this book
Use the elements that *inspire* you and *if you love them, do them again!*

Make time for yourself. *Commit to the pages*. Write in them, mark them, press flowers in them, doodle in them, record your thoughts in them and transform the pages into *your own*. Immerse yourself in the artwork. Let our Warrior Sisters help you to unfold your dreams and explore lost worlds. *Breathe, move and write...*

About us

Julie, *"I am a hair and make-up artist with a background in fashion. As a certified yoga teacher, what excites me is the way I see yoga transform women. Hair and make-up also change the way a woman feels about herself. You'll see me in the yoga poses throughout the book."*

Kate *"I am a graphic designer, illustrator and aerial dance teacher. I love creating inspiring artwork that takes the audience to beautiful new worlds. In this book, you'll see me on my aerial hoop in the trees of Rosslyn Glen, Edinburgh."*

The artwork

We have created this book in an unusual way, starting with the images first and accompanying them with our poetry and words.

We took great pleasure in the entire creative process; finding the locations, making the costumes, creating the sets and taking the photos whenever (and wherever) we could. We hope that the beauty of the artwork will inspire you to go on your own journey with your Warrior self.

*The Warrior Sisters pictured in this book are our friends. We chose each of them for their unique strengths and personalities. They are **real women** with their own incredible qualities. Their raw beauty shines through. There's been no photoshopping out their shapely curves, lines or blemishes.*

We are very grateful for the help of our photographers who were happy to give us total creative freedom in our beautiful but challenging Scottish locations. This book was self-funded so we also took many of the photos ourselves.

The yoga

Perhaps you haven't done yoga before in which case we recommend you **try a class,** or one-to-one tuition. It's really beneficial to have guidance from an experienced instructor when you are starting out.

The postures chosen in this book are **aligned with each Warrior Sister** and the emotion she represents. As with any posture, it is a good idea to warm up first with some sun salutations and gentle stretches in whatever way **feels good for your body.**

Yoga and aerial dance allow small, **powerful changes in your body** that bring you to a more empowered and conscious state.

Through our teaching, we have seen first hand how yoga and aerial dance have a knock-on effect, fostering growth and **abundance** in other areas of life for our students.

It is our belief that doing one posture for two minutes is more effective for the **mind and body** connection than racing quickly through lots of postures.

To you

We are all imperfect,
*some of us are luckier than others,
and some people have a very hard time.*

The Warrior Sisters *encourage us to stop beating
ourselves up, from making comparisons or striving
for unreal perfection! Each story brings a* **remedy.**
*Why don't you invite them in for a cup
of tea, or even something stronger.
Give them space. Give them your* **attention.**
In their **strength** *and vulnerability is the
medicine to awaken and inspire us.*

Show up for yourself,
*steal the moment "inbetween" to express yourself
in these pages and connect with your
own Warrior Sister. Shout out,
be curious, notice and find
your stillness.*

*Julie, Kate
& The Warrior Sisters*

"Imagination is the only weapon
in the war against reality."

"How puzzling all these changes are!
I'm never sure what I'm going to be, from one
minute to another."
Lewis Carroll, Alice in Wonderland

NAI VETY

*& the **Dreamer***

Fearless
don't blink

As the sky turns
ears quiver
taller than grass

One jump out of reach

Spirited
she follows
eyes wide
hot tempered
head strong

Fall down
muddy kneed
get up again

Hare darts
dirt tracks
...who are you?

Round in circles
whisper the wise
who cares?

This is where
dreams begin
hold your breath...

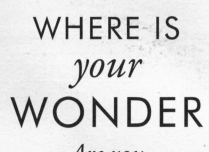

WHERE IS
your
WONDER

Are you

Busy chasing a hare?
Lost in mundane tasks?
Do you feel like you're going round in circles?
What is the purpose of your life,
is it just to get through each day?

What makes your heart sing
and your soul dance?

"We both had issues with schooling and didn't fit in.
Julie left school aged 15 and Kate failed to get into art school.
We both found other paths to reach our dreams." Julie & Kate

What *dreams* or ambitions did NOT
show up in your life so far?

List here those lost *dreams...*

_____

_____

_____

_____

_____

_____

What dream is IMPORTANT *to you now?*
How could you take a small action towards this dream today?

_____

_____

_____

Now make a *promise* to take one step, each week, towards your dream.
I promise

_____

_____

_____

Signed ....

Tame your HARE

Do this through statements you make to yourself. We call them Soul Statements but they are also called affirmations. They have been used for centuries in various forms, from mantras to prayers.

This is a way to connect to your subconscious mind, planting new thoughts. Powerful statements help you to keep your mind from going in negative circles. Here are some examples:

Dreams find me in curious ways.
Golden opportunities are everywhere.
I have unlimited potential as only good lies before me.
I am radiant and energetic. Life loves me.

1 _____

2 _____

3 _____

Feel the vibration of each word in your heart and pay close attention. Try to voice each word and listen with care. You will know which words feel right and which resonate with you.

BRIDGE

Setu Bandha Sarvangasana

Open the heart
and wake up to wonder.

It can feel scary to
open up to our emotions,
but breath by breath we can wake up
to the world waiting for us.

Play with this pose.
Enjoy it like getting to
know a new friend, a warm
companionship.

Benefits of this pose:
Energising.
Rejuvenating.
Exhilarating.

"I find this pose gives me a lot of energy.
It makes me feel open, calm and free." Julie

*"At times you have to leave the city of your comfort
and go into the wilderness of your intuition,
what you discover will be wonderful, what you
discover will be yourself."*
Alan Alda

"In a dark time the eye begins to see."
Theodore Roethke

INTU
ITION

& the Crow Queen

Change is coming
feel her in your gut
a scent, a shiver

She flies ahead
calls back to us

Dream shadows
unbearable
at times

Catch her
in the corner
of your eye...

In small places
in a whisper
among the dust

Ink the feather
...hear her caw

Be *still*
& LISTEN
to the inkling or small voice within.

She may whisper, leave a feeling...
and you will know what is right.

Can you listen without judgement?
The more we practice listening, the easier it will
become to trust our intuition.

We can sometimes confuse ourselves by asking
advice from others, when often the
answer lies within us.

The writing, breathing and
mindfulness exercises in this book
will help connect you to your
instinct and intuition.

*"Intuition is the one thing I wanted to teach Robyn, my daughter, to listen to.
I have told her and her friends of times when I have ignored
my gut instinct and put myself in danger." Kate*

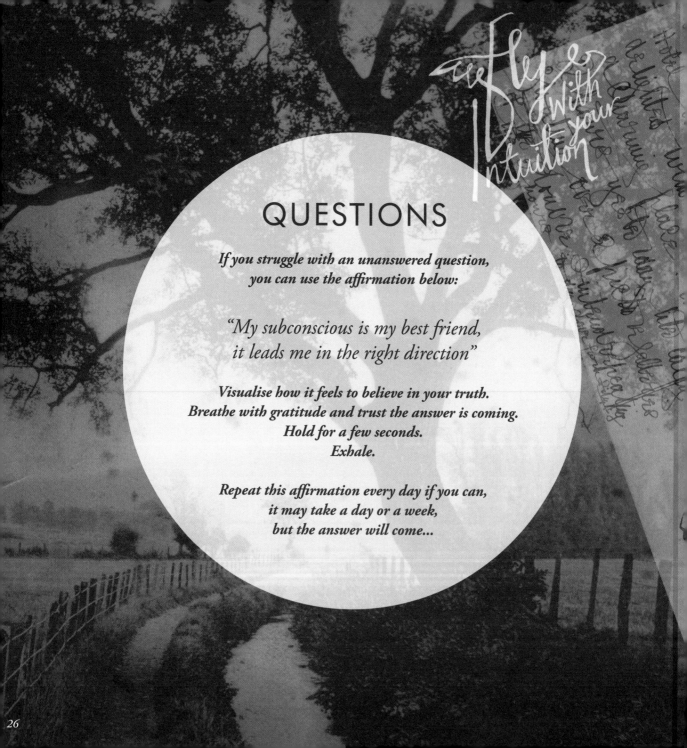

QUESTIONS

*If you struggle with an unanswered question,
you can use the affirmation below:*

*"My subconscious is my best friend,
it leads me in the right direction"*

*Visualise how it feels to believe in your truth.
Breathe with gratitude and trust the answer is coming.
Hold for a few seconds.
Exhale.*

*Repeat this affirmation every day if you can,
it may take a day or a week,
but the answer will come...*

A good way to tap into your intuition is to write a letter to yourself.
Imagine how your wise self in the future may respond.

Published by Dearden and Wade Bournemouth

Greetings

POST CARD

Question...

_____

_____

_____

_____

_____

Write the question and then take a few deep breaths and write your
answer, or sleep on it and answer in the morning.

Carte Postale

Correspondance   Adresse

Modèle   Dépose

My reply...

_____

_____

_____

_____

_____

_____

_____

27

LOTUS *Padmasana*

Close your eyes softly.
Turn your attention inside.
Palms face up to receive energy.
Thumb and finger can touch to help you focus.

Feel your breath come in...
Pause and gently allow the breath to flow back out.

To help calm the chatter of your mind, focus on
your breath. When the mind wanders bring your
attention to the breath again as if gently guiding
a child back in the right direction.

There is no rush to achieve a lotus position.
Cross your legs where they are comfortable,
or use a chair or cushion to sit upright.
Respect your body.

Listen to your intuition...

Benefits of this pose:
Opens the hips and stretches the spine.
Strengthens the nervous system.
Calms the mind.

How do you feel when you are still?
Do you feel distracted by an itch or is there a little discomfort?
Can you soften and allow it to be there? Do you feel blissful,
agitated or somewhere inbetween? Give yourself this magical space.

"If all you can do is crawl, start crawling."
Rumi

*"Relax into your suffering, relax through it rather
than escape or numb it."*
Herbert Benson

"Turn to the sun and let the shadows fall behind."
Maori Proverb

SHOCK
& the Ice Banshee

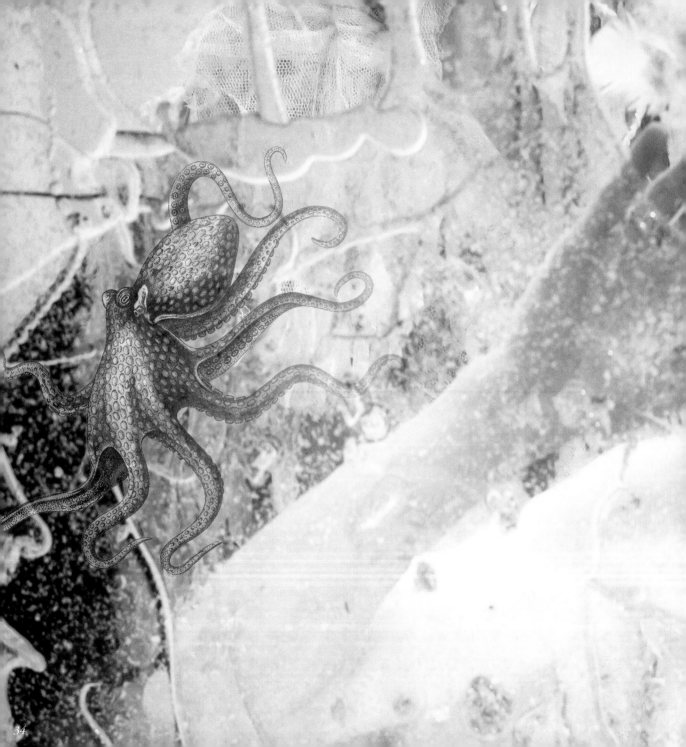

Pulled under
blue lips scream
a primal song

But
the air
has been stolen

A whirlpool
of frenzied
bones

Chill sets in
sinking deep
numb

Rest now...

It's too cold
for the soul
to dwell too long

As the light
finds its way
through the cracks

She will thaw
and laugh
again

After winter
spring
always comes…

Now is the
TIME
to take good care of yourself.
Indulge your needs and wishes.

In shock we cannot simply move on.
We may never be the same again.

There are no shortcuts. Grief that is held off will
often find its way back, It takes time to
face the grief we carry.

Without analysing or judging, can you
softly bring attention to your grief?
Can you be still, be present and simply breathe?

Treat yourself as you would treat a small child,
with tenderness and patience.

"This time too shall pass..."

"I was in shock when they switched off the life support machine for my Dad. I remembered his words from the time I was in a bad way and hadn't laughed or slept properly for a year. He said "you will thaw out and laugh again." Julie

SOUL VITAMINS

*Here are some suggestions of ways to
be kind to yourself when you are ready.
It is helpful to have a personal list to help you when you are
feeling overwhelmed. We call these Soul Vitamins.
Have a look at this list of things that helped us and people we know.*
FILL *your jar* opposite with a list of your own *Soul Vitamins.*

A walk with someone you trust, a change of surroundings.

Speaking to someone who makes you feel uplifted.

Playing your favourite music loudly to break the ice, help you thaw out and be present.

A warm bath with 10-15 drops of relaxing and balancing oils such as rose, geranium and lavender.

Surrounding yourself in warmth, soft lighting, candles, incense; whatever allows you to feel warm.

Taking a homeopathic remedy or a Bach Rescue Remedy.

Massage, acupuncture or reflexology.

Walking in nature and simple fresh air.

1 _____

2 _____

3 _____

4 _____

5 _____

PLOUGH *Halasana*

Heal yourself head to toe.

The spine should be warmed up first.
Begin by giving yourself a warm hug.

You can just enjoy the gentle roll on your
spine before you find this shape,
it may not be the full plough today!

If you need to rest more try Shavasana or child's pose.

Can you find the hidden treasure of your inner strength?

This posture is often taught before
or after a shoulder stand.

Take some nice long deep breaths.
Feel the earth supporting you.
Soften where you feel rigid.

Benefits of this pose:
Stretches the spine and reduces fatigue.
Keeps the immune system in good health.
Nourishes the heart.

"In these postures the world is turned upside down.
If we can get used to these feelings and changes on the mat,
it will help us to adapt to unexpected emotions." Kate

"As a fire blazes brightly when the covering of ash over it
is scattered by the wind, the divine fire within the body
shines in all its majesty when the ashes of desire
are scattered by the practice of pranayama."
B.K.S Iyengar

"She's mad, but she's magic. There's no lie in her fire."
Charles Bukowski

ANGER

& the *Twin* of *Kali*

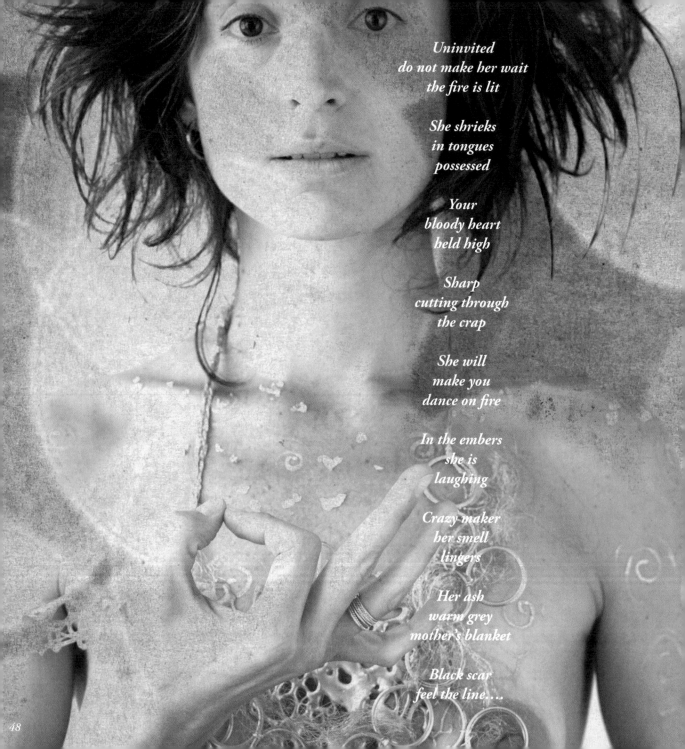

Uninvited
do not make her wait
the fire is lit

She shrieks
in tongues
possessed

Your
bloody heart
held high

Sharp
cutting through
the crap

She will
make you
dance on fire

In the embers
she is
laughing

Crazy maker
her smell
lingers

Her ash
warm grey
mother's blanket

Black scar
feel the line....

FEEL *the line*

Take time to look at what you are angry about.
We need anger, it helps us draw
boundaries for ourselves.

Listen to anger. She screams when we betray ourselves.
Do not stifle her, mask her, medicate or sedate her.
Use her power and channel the anger.
She points out those places that need our attention.

To get you out of your head and into your body,
can you feel the air?
As you breathe in, the air is cool.
As you breathe out, it is warm and moist...

*"I was so angry one day and my son came in and got me to smash an old plate
in the yard... a thing I always got my kids to do when they were very angry.
I laughed when my daughter came back from university with no plates
from doing the same with her friends!" Kate*

RANT & RAGE PAGE

*What am **I** ANGRY about?*

1

_____
_____
_____
_____
_____
_____
_____
_____
_____
_____
_____
_____
_____
_____
_____
_____
_____

If you don't want to write down your RANT
record it on your phone or type it out then
after a few breaths slowly delete it.
Or you can write on paper and burn it.

What do I not accept?
How does this show my boundaries?

_____
_____
_____
_____
_____
_____

2

3

*What can I do to move forward
now or next time....*

Now _____
_____

Later _____
_____
_____
_____
_____

4

*What will I have to accept
in this moment?*

_____
_____
_____
_____
_____
_____

*Sometimes when you feel
powerless and there is no
action you can take, try
a ritual of writing the
situation on paper and
freezing it in ice.*

TWIST
Ardha Matsyendrasana

Twist can take you
out of your mind and into your body.
Feel the discomfort, can you let it transform you?
Are you able to create a space for yourself
to just be, without any judgement?

Can you surrender to the feeling?
Use your breath as a reminder that it is not what
angers you now, it is how you react.

One breath at a time imagine
you are twisting all your anger out of your liver.

As you look over your shoulder see
if you can look at your anger from
a different angle.

Benefits of this pose:
Nourishes the heart.
Keeps the nervous system in good health.

*Some breathing practices that help release tension from
anger are Lions Breath, Ujjayi Breath of Fire,
Sheetali Pranayama and Sitali Pranayama.*

*"After a journey through the wilderness which
no one can make for us, which no one can spare us,
for our wisdom is the point of view from which at last
we come to view the world."*
Proust

*"My barn having burned to the ground,
I can now see the moon."*
Japanese poet Masahide

"The wound is the place where the light enters you."
Rumi

FUCK
IT

& Fionn the Warrior

Be
CONSCIOUS
What are you hungry for?

This moment may not
be full of yoga and green smoothies!
It may be a whisky and coke, a cigarette or a strong coffee,
but don't beat yourself up. Smoke or drink consciously
without judging yourself right now.

The future and the past can feel terrifying.
See that in this moment in time you are safe.
Can you release something that has been binding you?

Our stories or traumas and the way we hold on
to them can often run the show.

So, what is your story?

*"After two years recovering from a dark depression while working full time in a hair
salon in Edinburgh, I asked for a month off to go to India and was refused.
I thought 'fuck it.' I got the ticket, left my job and went to India to practise
Mysore with Sri K Pattabhi Jois for three months." Julie*

Wall of *multi-coloured* wounds

A wound is something that keeps you stuck, something you may think defines you or makes you feel like a victim. It is our advice to seek the guidance of a professional therapist if your state of mind needs more help.

Here is a useful step to help you move out of the victim mindset by re-writing your story in a light that shows your strength rather than your weakness or wound. Have you gained any wisdom through your own trauma? We can use our wounds as triggers to fight back and take a new and powerful stance.

A few words about my wound

My new empowered story

Tune into a different channel
turn down the volume and up the bass!

Your PLAYLIST...

CORPSE *Shavasana*

*Can you
wind down and stop?*

Can you bathe in the stillness?

Can you stop striving, just for a short time?

The Corpse is the most challenging posture.

*Let go of every part
of you, just say
"Fuck it this is my time
to give to myself."*

Benefits of this pose:
Rests our entire nervous system.
It's like re-booting your computer.
The death in this practice is as important as the birth.

"A good quality Shavasana is better than nine hours sleep because the sensory nervous system is completely at rest." Julie

"Why stop dreaming when you wake up."
Neil Gaiman

"Sometimes you wake up. Sometimes the fall kills you.
And sometimes, when you fall, you fly."
Neil Gaiman

"Play is the highest form of research."
Albert Einstein

PLAY

& the *Roseline Nymph*

Look closely…

In the
hollow
kissed scraps

Feet fae
nature's
old roots

Veined
wings catch
her light

As
mischief
makes

Other
worlds
wake

Infectious
wise child
nymph

Come follow me…

PLAY
Not just for kids

Play is a way to explore ourselves.
Can you do something you once loved to do?
Can you involve your senses?

Smell
Taste
Sound
Touch
Sight

Collect something shiny, or colourful (or not).
Experiment with your hair or clothes.
Revisit your childhood haunts.

"As a child, my Mum made a trapeze as I said I was going to be a circus performer.
I grew up and didn't think it was a job in real life. I was excited to meet a
trapeze teacher in my late 20's and was hooked. I went on to perform, one
highlight being in the Hong Kong New Year procession. I teach aerial now!" Kate

Can you answer? *When I was a child I...*

imagined *I could* be
_____

wanted *to* own
_____

missed *the* chance *to*
_____

could *have tried*
_____

was very good *at*
_____

felt proud *of myself when*
_____

One *thing I could still try from* **above** *is*
_____

Ten *years from now I will look back and be happy that I*
_____

To be one step closer to this, today *I will*
_____
_____

Treasured
SCRAPS

Get a box or tin
for your treasures and
collect things you love over time.
Anything. This is a collection of things
that inspire you in some way.
It could be just the colour,
the texture, the scent,
a word, a button
or a shell...

DANCE *Natarajasana*

Let's dance!
The story of this posture
is dancing through the patterns
and cycles we have been stuck in.

This pose helps us to play with balance
and break free from the mundane.

It doesn't matter how many times you
lose balance, the fun is in the play.
Find the dancer inside.

Benefits of this pose:
Expresses creativity and focus.
Leaves you with a sense of invigoration.
Builds strength and flexibility.

*This posture is challenging but, even if your pose looks
a little different, don't judge your shape and
be playful and light with yourself.*

"Who looks outside, dreams;
who looks inside, awakes."
Carl Gustav Jung

"What screws us up the most in life is the
picture in our head of what it's supposed to be."
Jeremy Binns

"Life is amazing. And then it's awful. And then it's
amazing again. And in between the amazing and awful
it's ordinary and mundane and routine. Breathe in the
amazing, hold on through the awful, and relax and exhale
during the ordinary. That's just living heartbreaking,
soul-healing, amazing, awful, ordinary life.
And it's breathtakingly beautiful."
L.R. Knost

NOW

& the *Samadh-shakti*

Noise…

Traffic
amplified

Time was
promised

Shit, the fox
needs fed

What ye
raking fur?

She searches
the lost networks

Through
abandoned chaos

Steal the
moment

#EH6
defrag

84

STEAL THE
MOMENT

Do you find yourself overthinking things?
In this fast-paced modern world with a constant stream
of information, multi-tasking and social media,
it can be hard for us to truly relax and be still.
When you feel your brain spiraling with incessant chatter,
it is easy to feel overwhelmed, your inner voice always interrupting
and over-analysing... would you let a friend interrupt and judge
you every moment of the day? Didn't think so!

You have done well to notice this internal crazy chatter.
Don't take yourself personally!

Can you stop, breathe and reset your inner critic,
or do something that requires you to
engage your mind and pull
you into a different flow?

"My mind can be so busy so when I need to unplug I set my timer for 15 minutes and just
focus on my breathing. When the thoughts come, I try to just see them as clouds floating
past, allowing thoughts to be there but not getting hooked into them." Julie

IDENTIFY something that is cluttering up your head or worrying you.

Take a deep breath, inhale and exhale slowly to focus.

Continue with your breathing and place your attention on the ground beneath you. Look at it, take in every detail, acknowledge its colour and texture, then say "I see the ground."

Take another breath

As you exhale

Imagine taking your worry into your hand and throwing it as hard and far as you can, out into a distant junk yard.

With each following breath, imagine your worry being shattered, trashed and destroyed.

Then, come back to the ground below you. Feel it hold you, anchor you and support you. This is where you are right now and exactly where you need to be. In this moment, you are free from this worry.

If you want to learn more about transformational breathwork, try Nadi Shodhana Practice (alternate nostril breathing) to settle stress and help you feel clear and free.

TAKE

20

Calm, repetitive tasks can allow the brain to settle into a state of relaxation, requiring minimal effort or strain.

Turn your phone onto **silent** mode
and set a 20 minute timer.

Treat yourself to some creative pottering.
Do something repetitive and soothing, just one thing.
Rearrange a bookshelf into colour order,
do some gardening or fold some clothes.

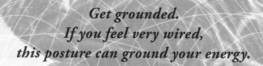

Get grounded.
If you feel very wired,
this posture can ground your energy.

You can imagine you have wires or roots
going down deep into the earth and a wire
from the sky lifting you from
the crown of your head.

Can you plug yourself into this moment?
Can you find your balance?
You can place your foot wherever it feels comfortable.
With practice you may manage two minutes
balancing on each leg. You can even gently
shut your eyes if you feel balanced enough.

Be here.
Breathe now.

Benefits of this pose:
Invigorates and rejuvenates.
Helps with concentration when you feel out of sorts.
Teaches you to be present in the moment.

Can you escape your busy mind?
A tree must be able to sway in the wind
yet be rooted down into the earth.

defrag.exe C: -f -v > "e:\doc\defrag report C.txt"
defrag.exe D: -f -v > "e:\doc\defrag report D.txt"
defrag.exe C: -f
defrag.exe D: -f

"The minute I heard my first love story,
I started looking for you, not knowing
how blind that was.
Lovers don't finally meet somewhere.
They're in each other all along."
Rumi

"As we let our own light shine, we unconsciously give other
people permission to do the same."
Marianne Williamson

"You yourself, as much as anybody in the entire universe,
deserve your love and affection."
Buddha

LOVE
& Mother ***O Na Lani***

Hummm

Born from
sea foam

Washed up
on warm air

Crystallised
in sunlight

Exhale

Sing to weeds
between cracks

Softly trace
each scar

Eyes feel
beyond walls

She smiles and
does her own thing

Just knowing…

LOVE

We live in a world
filled with judgement.
Can you accept yourself a little bit more?
How are you taking care of this moment?

When you notice you are
thinking negatively about yourself,
try not to cling on to the thought. Let it pass as clouds
pass by in the sky. Find a new thought that's more
uplifting, and stick with it, even if it is
just for that moment.

Over time it becomes easier to just notice
and not get caught up in the critic inside you.
Mother yourself.

Can you imagine what is possible
for the life about to be born?

*"I always used to look for love and validation from other people.
I came to realise to find real love I first needed to feel love for myself and follow my own
groove. It's a constant challenge to keep my negative inner critic at bay!..." Kate*

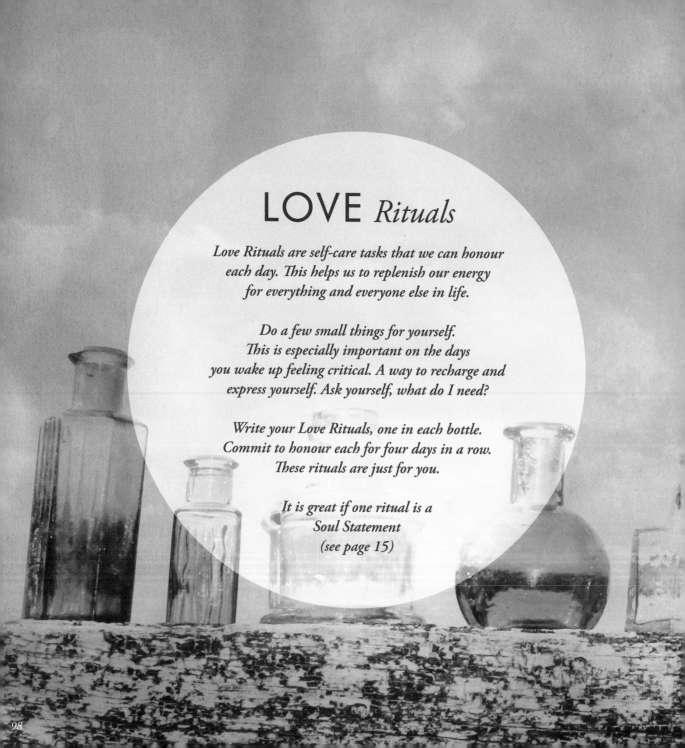

LOVE *Rituals*

*Love Rituals are self-care tasks that we can honour
each day. This helps us to replenish our energy
for everything and everyone else in life.*

*Do a few small things for yourself.
This is especially important on the days
you wake up feeling critical. A way to recharge and
express yourself. Ask yourself, what do I need?*

*Write your Love Rituals, one in each bottle.
Commit to honour each for four days in a row.
These rituals are just for you.*

*It is great if one ritual is a
Soul Statement
(see page 15)*

Some suggestions:

Skin brushing

*A hot bath with candles
and essential oils*

Soul Statements

Daily meditation

*Hot water and lemon
in the morning*

Super smoothie

Stretching for 10 minutes

*A yoga posture
Shavasana (see page 64)*

*Dance for five minutes to
your favourite song*

BOW
Urdhva Dhanurasana

Like an archer's bow,
we want to be supple and strong
so our arrows of intention can
soar high and help us to manifest love.

This posture allows us to be
vulnerable but conquer our fears.
A great warm up for Bridge pose (see page16)

Maintain a strong intention.
Unwavering commitment.
Open the heart to
receive love.

Benefits of this pose:
Relieves stress, opens the heart.
Energises the body and strengthens your spine.
Improves internal balance and harmony in the body.

*"If you can't catch your ankles
don't worry. With long socks on the toes,
catch the end of the socks instead."* Kate

A DATE *with yourself*

*This is one of our favourite tasks but very hard to do.
The idea is to make time for yourself. See how your relatives,
children or friends need you, just when you are about to make this time!
Think of it as if you were meeting a new love for a date...
Would you stand them up?*

Rules

*Switch off your phone.
Only go alone (no gooseberries).
Do not run any errands for others on the way.*

*Your date with yourself can be just one hour doing something you love,
going somewhere special for an afternoon, or collecting for your
treasured scraps box (see page 75)*

Date:_____

Time:_____

"Surrender to what is.
Let go of what was.
Have faith in what will be."
Sonia Ricotti

"You will find that it is necessary to let things go;
simply for the reason that they are heavy. So let them
go, let go of them. I tie no weights to my ankles."
C.Joybell

We arrive into this world as energy, same as
stars, wildlife, wind and ocean. Messy, raw, and
continuously perfect in our chaos. Release the need to
control, and instead surrender to your own natural
rhythm, as expansive, accepting and open to new
circumstances and situations as air itself.
That is how you'll thrive."
Victoria Erickson

SURR
ENDER

& Yemaya of the Sea

Salt of the earth
kiss her hand

Grief's cradle
set to sea

A paper cut
the ink runs

So many
things

She wanted
to say

Does it matter
after all?

We can't tame
white horses…

SURRENDER
& Let go

You may have worked so hard to keep it all together,
now the work is to let it all go.

Throw each
word to the wind.
Unfold your wings.

When we have angry thoughts in
our heads we can offload them
into written words.
Then they become prisoners
on the paper and we can
let them go.

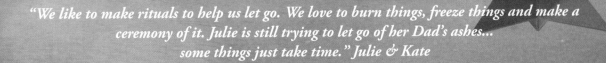

"We like to make rituals to help us let go. We love to burn things, freeze things and make a
ceremony of it. Julie is still trying to let go of her Dad's ashes...
some things just take time." Julie & Kate

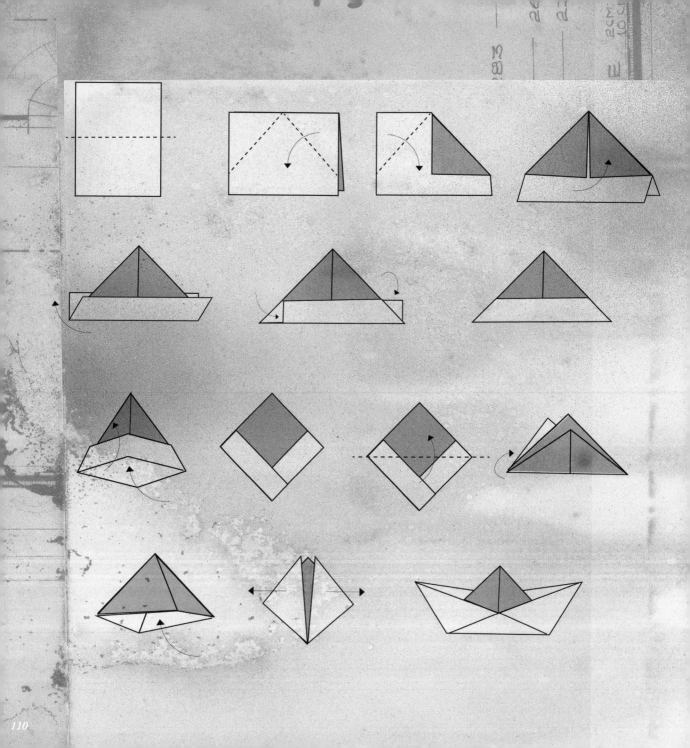

Surrender BOAT

Refusing to forgive someone or yourself imprisons a part of you. Can you allow the feeling to just be there? Can you soften around the feeling without getting caught up in the story?

On a sheet of A5 paper, write very specifically the name or situation that you want to surrender, forgive and move forward from.

Use that paper to make a boat (or you can just crunch the paper into a floating ball). As you fold the boat (or screw the paper up) repeat a Soul Statement such as...

"I forgive you, you forgive me"

Make a boat for yourself too, it is important to forgive yourself and let yourself off the hook.

In our experience we found that sometimes we need to surrender and forgive in layers. It may take time. Some folk may need a whole fleet of boats!

As you free your boat in water, breathe and feel each emotion that surfaces.

EAGLE *Garudasana*

Surrender
to the stretch.
The posture shown is
a preparation for the Eagle pose.

Go easy on yourself,
find a posture that suits you.
The journey is more important than the destination.

You may have days where you just want to
lie down on your yoga mat and this is ok.

What can you let go of and surrender today?

You could leave your mat unrolled next to your bed.
In the morning you can just roll on
to it for a few minutes.
Let go and find joy
in the stretch.

Benefits of this pose:
*Releases and strengthens hips and ankles.
Helps you to re-focus and refresh.
Good for circulation.*

"I used to judge myself if I couldn't do a pose. I realise now it's more important to achieve a state of stillness. That is where the real success lies, not in the shape of a posture." Julie

Surrender

*"I will not let anyone walk through my mind
with their dirty feet."*
Mahatma Gandhi

*"Love is much like a wild rose, beautiful and calm,
but willing to draw blood in its defense."*
Mark Overby

EMPOWER MENT

*& the **Bee Priestess***

I Am
a wild Rose
Beautiful and Calm
But willing to
Draw Blood
in
its Defense

Old Rose

Petals
guarded
by thorns

She burns
but is not
consumed

Moon
hive
star
gate

Her tears
turn to
bees

Each sting
opens
the line

A Rose-line

EMPOWER
Sting & Zing

Are you avoiding something
that makes you feel uncomfortable?
Are you afraid of speaking your mind?

Every sting is an opening,
to find your resilience.

Can you speak your truth or find the strength to deal
with what you have been avoiding?

Unfold your qualities and be brave.
Get out of your comfort zone
and hang in there.

"My bedroom window looked out to Rosslyn chapel over the field.
I think I knew on a deep level it was sacred, I could escape,
and there was a bigger power around to help me." Julie

Rose of EMPOWERMENT

What do you need to feel like you?
What are the important elements that enable you
to feel your life is in balance?

For example:
Relationships, family, friendships, home, creativity,
spirituality, health, self development, adventure,
travel, recognition, romance, passion.

Write 8 values, one in each of the circles opposite.

How much do you honour each value
with your time or energy?

Score each value by colouring in each segment from the
centre of the circle outwards.

This exercise can allow you to see how you
balance your time and energy in accordance
with your own values.

HORSE *Vatayanasana*

Shift your mood.
The horse pose builds heat in the body
and can be done at any time without
the need to warm up beforehand.

Along with warrior pose, this is an amazing power
posture that can be used to ignite your inner
strength. The next time you are about to go into a
stressful situation, such as an interview, do this in
the loo first. Aim for two minutes,
but 30 seconds will make a difference!

To give extra punch take a deep inhalation and
then say your Soul Statement as you exhale.
Feel the connection to the
earth through your feet.

Wake up your Warrior.

Benefits of this pose:
Strengthens the muscles in your legs.
Builds srength in the core and resilient knees.
Helps you feel alert.

Can you relax your mind and find strength in your body?
Practise with your back against a wall for support.

BRAMARI

Humming Bee Breath
Provides instant release in moments of frustration.
Calms the entire nervous system and offers
a quick pick-me-up for busy people!

Sit up straight.
Softly close your eyes.
Place your index fingers on the soft cartilage
of the ear to block the noise outside.
With lips lightly sealed, inhale through your nose.
As you exhale make the sound of the letter M,
essentially a humming sound. Do not force it but
sustain the sound until you need to inhale.
Repeat, inhale through the nose and then hum
like a buzzing bee when you exhale.

Try for eight hums or more if it feels good!
The longer you sustain the humming
exhalation, the more relaxing the
bee breath will be.

"Better to lose count while naming your blessings, than to lose your blessings to counting your troubles."
Maltbie D. Babcock

"Be soft. Do not let the world make you hard. Do not let the pain make you hate. Do not let the bitterness steal your sweetness. Take pride that even though the rest of the world may disagree, you still believe it to be a beautiful place."
Iain Thomas

"You've gotta ask yourself one question... 'Do I feel lucky?' Well, do ya, punk?"
Clint Eastwood

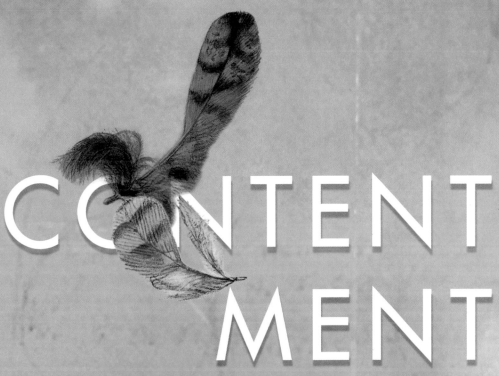

CONTENT MENT

& Sister Laxmi

Bare
foot
roller

Skater
mood
maker

Shining
shaman
sister

Drift
with
her

Wind
mills
sing

How
lucky
I am

CONTENTMENT
& Gratitude

Are you in too much pain to feel grateful?
Try saying "I accept what is and what is to come."
We can increase our contentment through the practice of
manifesting gratitude and feeling grateful
for what we already have.

Our gratitude must be authentic. Simple things such as
a warm bed, an abundance of food, a good friend,
or another day to start again.

Can you take some time to quietly recognise these
small but pivotal things? Focus on them and
record them in your own way.
See our favourite ways
to do this!

"Writing in our gratitude journal is something we love to do regularly and
feeling grateful is a power that never fails to amaze us. You don't have to do it
every day. Just as often as feels good for you." Kate & Julie

Golden lotus
VISUALISATION

Sit quietly and close your eyes softly.
Slowly and deeply breathe in through your nose.
Exhale slowly focusing on your breath and feel as if you
are breathing out from your heart.

Visualise a golden lotus flower in your heart.
Slowly and deeply breathe in through your nose.

Inhale *the feeling of love as the petals of the lotus open,*
then visualise a 'miniature you' sitting in the middle of the lotus.
Hold your breath *for the count of five seconds and slowly exhale.*
As you exhale the lotus petals
close around you.

Repeat until any
stress you feel dissolves
into love.

WHY *is gratitude so* POWERFUL?
A little GRATITUDE *test.*

Sit quietly and imagine a beautiful white feather.
Imagine how soft and how light it is, breathe in and out slowly and
say "thank you" for this feather as you imagine it.

Now write below (five times, slowly) thank you for this
beautiful white feather (or token of your choice)

1 _____

2 _____

3 _____

4 _____

5 _____

…Now just see what happens.
Yes, it is true there are white feathers everywhere, but rarely do we
take any notice. In our state of gratitude and in thanking them for
their existence, they begin to appear everywhere!

Gratitude brings a brighter vibration, lifts you and will multiply the
things you notice and are in tune with on a daily basis.
When you find your feather, keep it as a reminder and put it with
your treasured scraps. Could it be that the more good
you notice, the more you will find?

On this side
of the page,
begin each entry

"Thank you for"

for things you
feel
grateful for
right now.

As you write,
feel the gratitude
flow from your
heart
to the pen and
this page.

Thank you

49

On this side of the page, consider the future and what you would like your life to be like. What will you be grateful for in months or years to come?

Describe this gratitude in the *present* tense and visualise how good it feels to have these things and feel grateful for them.

Visualise yourself in this *future now* and express your gratitude. You will be amazed at what happens...

ANJALI *Mudra*

It's a brand new day
to start again.

Anjali Mudra is a centering pose.
It helps you to focus and bring clarity when
you feel a bit all over the place.
It harmonises the two
hemispheres of the brain.

The hands can be held at the heart,
brow or above the crown of your head.

This pose allows you to manifest
gratitude for this day.

Benefits of this pose:
Centres the mind.
Aligns the body.

"The palms together is often used as a greeting "Namaste" which means "the light in me bows to the light in you." Kate

Thank you jar

When nice
things happen,
write on bits of paper
and keep the notes in a jar.
You can create "Thank you in
advance" notes or "Thank you
now" notes. This is great to do
with kids. Young children can
draw a thank you picture.
Choose a special day
to open the jar.

"When the seeds of happiness in you are watered,
you will become happy. When the seed of anger in
you is watered, you will become angry.
The seeds that are watered frequently are
those that will grow strong."
Thich Nhat Hanh

'Your vision will become clear only when you look
into your heart.…..he who looks outside, dreams.
he who looks inside, awakens."
Carl Gustav Jung

UNDER
WORLD

& La Luna Selkie

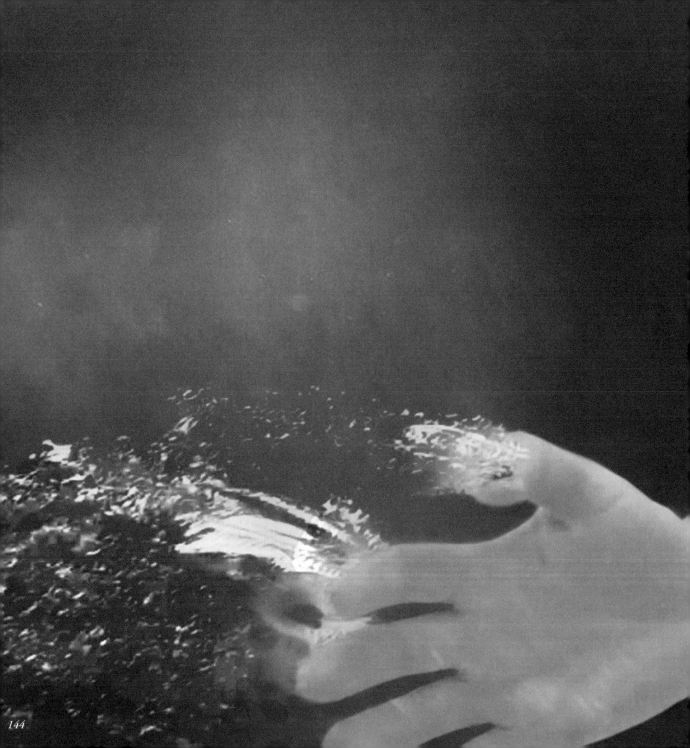

On lonely
stretches
hold tight

Your seal skin

Taste
the
salt

Surf
the
ride

Every
bone
bleached

The
depth
feeds

Lit up
the moon
sees itself

DIVE
a little deeper

Where do our thoughts and beliefs come from?
If we dive deeper what can we find?

What invisible roots grow beneath our busy minds?
What seeds of thought are we planting,
and how can we be a good friend and
be more gentle to ourselves?

We can dive deeper to uncover our own strength and
connect fully to ourselves through activities such as yoga,
meditation, journaling and igniting our creative side.

Sometimes we might need to enlist the help
of a professional counsellor
or therapist to go
a bit deeper.

"Before we wrote each Warrior Sister poem, Julie and I shared this ritual.
We set an alarm for ten minutes and focussed on one Warrior Sister with our eyes closed.
Then we silently wrote and sketched our thoughts in a mind map
before sharing them with eachother." Kate & Julie

ROOT MAP

*Use this Root Map to find the roots of your thoughts
and set new seeds of intention for your future.*

*Your mind is like a garden and we can plant many different kinds
of thoughts or seeds, the wholesome and the harmful ones,
seeds of joy, anger, gratitude, grief or bitterness.
What seeds do we want to cultivate and grow?*

*Use the Root Map to choose a purposeful action, to set an intention.
Map your thoughts on how to get there. In words or pictures,
plant ideas to take you in your own direction.*

My intention is..............................

The seed I plant is...........................

List of things that helped us
DIVE *deeper*

Yoga
Pranayana
Aerial dance
Acupunture
Visualisation
Hypnotherapy
Homeopathy
Emotional Freedom Technique (EFT)

BOOKS
The Artist's Way by Julia Cameron
Creative Visualization by Shakti Gawaind
Women Who Run With The Wolves by Clarissa Pinkola Estés
Yoga Mala by Shri K.Pattabhi Jois
Light on Yoga by B.K.S. Iyengar

*Beneath
the surface exists
our own unique
strengths, our*
WARRIOR
*Selves
where we can plant
fresh seeds and grow
new roots.*

CAMEL *Ustrasana*

Bridge the gap
between body and mind.

Backbending triggers deep emotions,
opening up to your vulnerability.
A journey into the underworld, shining a torch
onto the darker parts of yourself.

Don't compromise your body.
Even a slight backbend using a wall for support
will be a great way to begin.

Close your eyes
and surrender.

Benefits of this pose:
Boosts mood.
Energises the body.

"What do backbends bring to you? Anger, sadness, panic or freedom?
For me, after I suffered a brain haemorrhage it took years
of courage to work through my vulnerability and release my neck backwards." *Julie*

NAIVETY *& the Dreamer*

MODEL *Robyn Vick (Kate's daughter)* **PHOTOGRAPHER** *Kate & Julie*

LOCATION *The gate location is in West Lothian, Edinburgh, as is the field. We had a really hard job getting out of the field in Julie's little car, backing up out of the mud onto a main road. Robyn was so patient with us.*

INTUITION *& the Crow Queen*

MODEL *Numba Pinkerton* **PHOTOGRAPHER** *Anna Isola Crolla*

LOCATION *Anna Isola Crolla's studio. Anna is Julie's close friend and a fashion photographer. Here Julie felt free to be creative with her styling. Anna and her sister, Maria, always made everyone so comfortable and fed us with Italian cooking.*

SHOCK *& the Ice Banshee*

MODEL *Magdalena Durant* **PHOTOGRAPHER** *Kate & Julie*

LOCATION *Magdelena's photographs were taken in Out of the Blue Drill Hall in Leith, Edinburgh where we both have our studios. Magdelena spent a lot of time on the cold concrete floor!*

ANGER *& the Twin of Kali*

MODEL *Marta Serrano* **PHOTOGRAPHER** *Robert Duyf / Kate, Julie & Marta*

LOCATION *The Bimhuis, an old Jazz club in Amsterdam. The twin picture was taken by Roberto. He said to Julie 'grab a potato' and they painted it red for the heart. The masked image was taken in an Ayurvedic Healing Centre in Amsterdam.*

FUCK IT *& Fionn the Warrior*

MODEL *Kaisia Zawadzka* **PHOTOGRAPHER** *Stuart McClay*

LOCATION *St Peter's Seminary, a disused Roman Catholic seminary near Cardross, Argyll and Bute, Scotland. It has been abandoned since 1980. We all had to squeeze through a tiny window in the ruin with all our kit to access the site.*

PLAY *& the Rosslyn Nymph*

MODEL *Kate George* **PHOTOGRAPHER** *Sean Inglis*

LOCATION *Rosslyn Glen. Julie lived in Rosslyn an a child and used to play by the sweet chestnut tree which is over 800 years old. The light was incredible. As Kate danced on her hoop, it shone through the trees in a truly magical way.*

NOW *& Samadh-shakti*

MODEL *Nikki Kilburn* PHOTOGRAPHER *Kate & Julie*

LOCATION *Dalton Scrap Metal Yard. Famous for featuring in the film Trainspotting and to local people in Leith for its massive rats! Nikki was so brave to be naked in this environment. Nikki works in mental health, specialising in trauma recovery work.*

LOVE *& Mother O Na Lani*

MODEL *Annalese McDermott* PHOTOGRAPHER *Stuart McClay*

LOCATION *Dunbar, Edinburgh. We took all our lamps and props to a friend's house, with its beautiful, hand-washed, green walls. On the way back in our hired van, a spray can of red paint exploded. To our relief a precious chaise longue was unscathed!*

SURRENDER *& Yemaya of the Sea*

MODEL *Mary Moriarty* PHOTOGRAPHER *Susie Lowe*

LOCATION *On the beautiful Seacliff beach, East Lothian. Mary just danced through the waves, despite sinking into the sand and almost falling in the sea in October. Mary is an inspiration and such fun!*

EMPOWERMENT *& the Bee Priestess*

MODEL *Sarah Pritchard* PHOTOGRAPHER *Euan Myles*

LOCATION *Rosslyn Chapel. In the roof are ancient havens created for bees. The stone roses above are associated with female wisdom. Inscribed on the apprentice pillar is "wine is strong, a king is stronger, women are even stronger, but truth will conquer all."*

CONTENTMENT *& Sister Laxmi*

MODEL *Tory Hyndman* PHOTOGRAPHER *Kate & Julie*

LOCATION *Tory's lovely Ayurvedic Healing Centre in Amsterdam. We made the costume the night before and cycled along the canals with it the next morning. Tory's children were there and were keen to have their photo taken too!*

UNDER WORLD *& La Luna Selkie*

MODEL *Mairi McLellan* PHOTOGRAPHER *Janeanne Gilchrist / Kate & Julie*

LOCATION *Pond image at Gosford house, Scotland, with the talented Janeanne. Permission for underwater photography was refused at every pool. So Kate and Julie just chanced it, armed with Mairi and a Go Pro at a local outdoor swimming pool.*

We would like to thank our models,
who in order to get into the soul of their Warrior
Sister, have been baptised in the Scottish seas, smeared
with dirt, inhaled smoke, sat in rat infested rubbish,
squeezed through no access gates, pressed against stone
pillars wearing only lace, been dragged barefoot
through fields and splatted with paint.

Thank you also to our photographers who have
plunged into stagnant ponds, squeezed through holes
in walls and been blown around in the
unpredictable Scotish weather.

Thank you to Nawa Jyoti for being an
inspirational yoga teacher and helping with
the yoga sections. Thank you to Nikki Kilburn for
putting us on the right track with our poetry.
Thank you to Abi Titterington-Lough and Laura Wood
for checking and proofing so patiently.

Thank you to Sean and Alex for being such amazing
partners on our journey in creating this book. Thank
you to our children Robyn, Joe and Enki and to our
families and friends who support us so much.

Thank you for reading this.
We honour the Warrior in you.

Kate & Julie